WHY DADDY SERVES HIS COUNTRY

• • • • • •

a MILITARY HISTORY COLORING BOOK

story by
R. SCOTT PRICE, MAJOR, USA & SCOTT NOVZEN

edited by
ROBERT G. SEGEL

original line art by
SCOTT NOVZEN

layout
BENJAMIN SIDON

published by
CHIPOTLE PUBLISHING, LLC
180 Cassia Way, #508
Henderson, NV 89014
702.565.0746 Fax 702.558.1728
www.smallarmsoftheworld.com

printed in China through Colorcraft Ltd., Hong Kong

The fall afternoon was warm with a cool breeze that flowed through her long rusty-colored hair. It was exactly the kind of day that young Molly Reese loved when she rode her bike to and from school. She couldn't pedal as fast as she usually did because her little brother Jimmy was doing his best to keep up.

When they rode into their home's driveway they noticed that their father's truck was already parked in the family's garage. That meant that their Daddy had come home from work early - something he rarely, if ever, did. Molly knew something was up and hoped everything was OK.

Molly and Jimmy parked their bikes and entered the house through the family room. Walking in they noticed that Daddy's Army uniform and equipment were laying on the chair. They sensed something was up. Mom looked like she had been crying. She cleared her throat and announced that Daddy has a very important announcement to make.

Daddy asked the kids to sit around him and said, "You kids know that I am a sergeant in our state's National Guard, and that sometimes I have to put on my uniform and boots and go help people. Well, some people in another part of the world have asked for help and I have been told by my bosses in the Army that we need to pitch in to help them."

Molly asked, "How long will you be gone this time Daddy, and when do you have to leave?"

"I'll be gone for about a year and I'll be leaving in a couple of weeks."

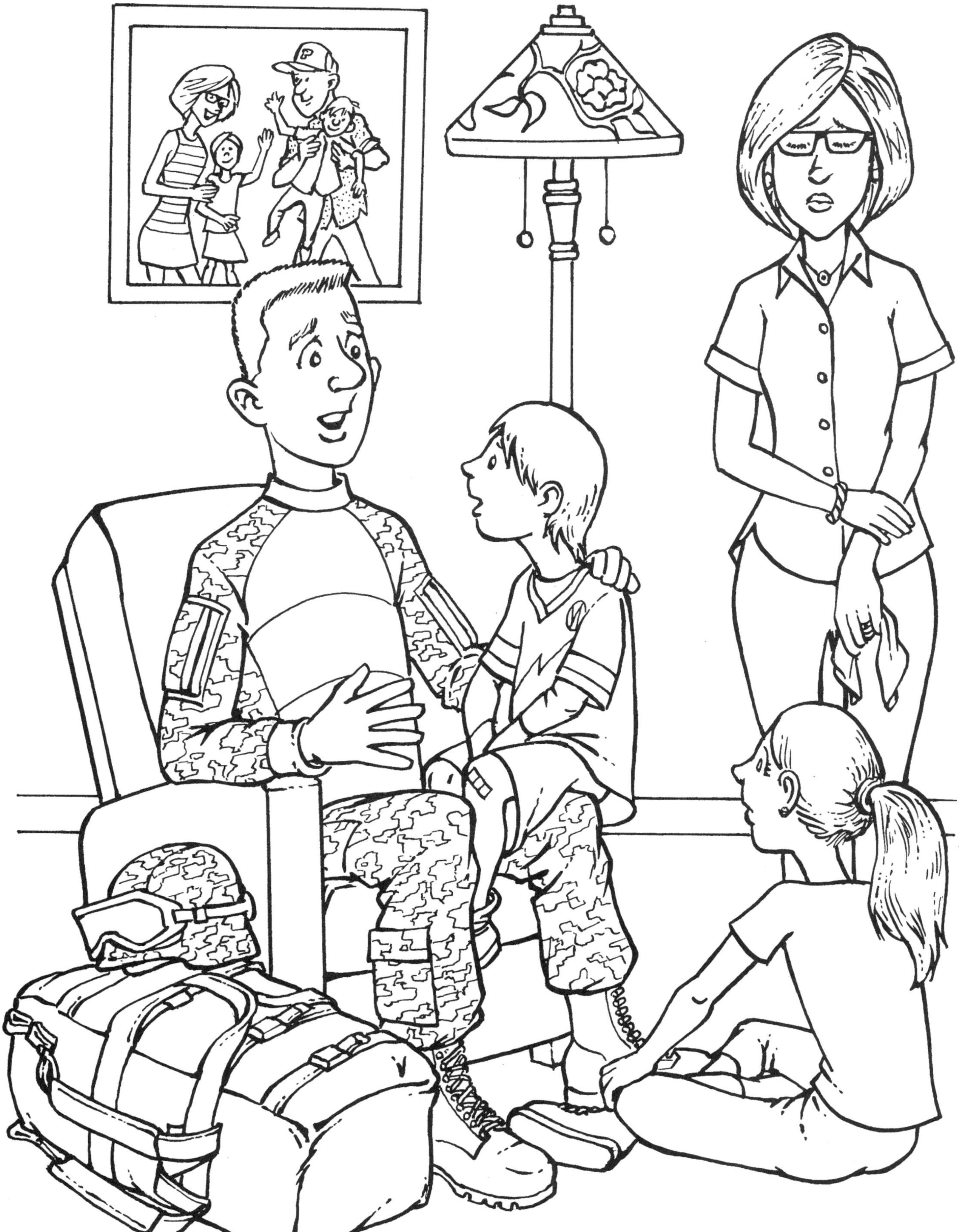

"A whole year?" Jimmy asked. "But what about Christmas and our camping vacation in Arizona next summer?"

Molly noticed that her Mom had looked away and was wiping tears off of her cheeks. Then she asked, "Daddy, you'll miss my graduation and my school play and who's going to coach our soccer team?"

"Mom can video tape them and send them to me," Daddy said with a sigh. "It won't be as good as being there with you but at least I won't miss them completely and we will just have to wait a while for our trip to the Grand Canyon."

Molly, sitting cross-legged at Dad's feet then asked, "Why do you have to go and help? "Can't somebody else who is not a Daddy go?"

"No honey, I'm afraid not," he replied. "It is very important that women and men just like me pitch in and help out. Remember a few years ago when we had the flood and all of us soldiers filled and stacked sand-bags to keep the river from flooding our town? And last summer when my platoon had to go and help fight forest fires up in the Rocky Mountains?"

"Yes, Daddy, I remember that."

"Well, this is even more important," Daddy replied. "A lot of people are counting on us and this might be the most important thing I am ever asked to do."

"Why Daddy?" they both said in unison.

75
U.S. ARMY

"Do you know how there are a couple of mean kids at your school who pick on you sometimes?" he asked.

"You mean bullies, Daddy?" asked Molly.

"Yes," He replied. "There are bullies in the grown up world too, and somebody has to stand up and stop them from hurting other people. Some very mean and bad men have been hurting some innocent people for a very long time and I am going to help stop those bullies. The people we are helping, especially their children, are afraid all of the time and we are going to protect them and keep them safe and teach them about freedom so that they take care of themselves in the future and stand up to the bullies on their own."

"Honey, our family has always been in the thick of things when bullies tried to hurt our families and friends, right from the very start of our country," Daddy answered. "Your Uncle Bill is serving in the Army right now helping guard the people who live in South Korea protecting them from bad men. Your mom's sister, Aunt Maggie, was a pilot during Operation Desert Storm. When a bully country attacked tiny Kuwait, to steal its oil, Aunt Maggie and friends from here and other countries fought to help those people. Today they are living free. They're gladly willing to do their part for what is right."

"My Dad, your grandpa, served as a crewman on a river patrol boat in what they called the Brown Water Navy. They fought to keep the invaders from the North from destroying their country of South Vietnam," Daddy said sadly.

"Is that how Pop Pop lost his hand? I thought that he got hurt on the farm."

"Yes princess, at a place called the Mekong Delta."

"But Daddy, all those stories are from before I was even born. What does it have to do with us?" Molly asked.

"We're here today living in the United States of America because before any of us were born, men and women stood up to bullies and told them 'enough was enough,'" he said. "If it hadn't been for them we wouldn't be here today living in a free country."

NAVY

"Honey, nobody likes to fight but sometimes trouble comes looking for you and there is no choice except to defend yourself. Like my Dad used to tell me when I was a little boy, 'freedom is never free.' Most of our ancestors were not born to be soldiers," Daddy continued. "Heck most of them were farmers or mechanics or kids fresh out of school - if they were lucky enough to even go to school. But when their country called them to duty they willingly went."

"Pop Pop's Dad, your Great Grandpa, served as a Marine in World War II fighting in the Pacific islands against the Japanese who had attacked our country without any warning. The fighting was terrible but Americans, along with soldiers, sailors and airmen from Great Britain, Australia, New Zealand, India, China and some other allied countries fought the Japanese and drove them from the islands they had invaded and conquered for over 5 long years."

USMC
51

"His brother Earl, your Great Uncle, was a 19-year old boy who served as a medic in Europe and saw action in the cold of winter in Belgium at the Battle of the Bulge and later the invasion of Germany. He was one of the first medical personnel to enter a horrible place called Dachau where evil men and women killed thousands of innocent people, most just because of their religious beliefs," Daddy said softly. "Molly, he had nightmares of his experiences for the rest of his life. What he saw there proves for all time that good men and women must do whatever it takes to stand up to bullies."

310 ★
HQ 1

"Your Great Great Grand Father on your Mom's side of the family, Hector, served as a soldier, or 'Doughboy' as they were called, in the First World War. He fought in the trenches as a member of the Army's hard charging 79th Division as a BAR gunner, way back in 1918. During the last week of the war he was hurt by German poison gas and suffered from lung problems until the day he died, nearly forty years later. He took great satisfaction that he was a citizen soldier and proudly wore his old uniform and medals when marching in each Veteran's Day parade."

US

"His father, Nathan, served as an officer under a general named John 'Blackjack' Pershing with the famous 10th Cavalry, or as they were known, the 'Buffalo Soldiers,'" Daddy continued. "These black men served in the Army as enlisted soldiers and during the Spanish-American War with Spain they helped capture the forts during the famous charge up San Juan Hill in Cuba along with Colonel Teddy Roosevelt and his Rough Riders. Teddy Roosevelt later became the 26th President of the United States. He always thought it was a crying shame that those Rough Riders got all the credit when in fact the 10th Cavalry Regiment did most of the fighting up the hill that day."

"During the War Between the States, two of my ancestors, brothers Edward and John Reese, fought on opposite sides: one for the North the other for the South. They both served in the cavalry and at a place called Gettysburg their units actually fought each other with pistols and sabers. Both brothers survived the four years of war but each lost a leg... Edward his right one and John his left. After the war they became very close again and, as luck would have it, they both had the same shoe size. So each year they would take the train to Richmond together and buy a pair of shoes."

"That's kind of sad and funny at the same time, Daddy," said Molly with a twinkle in her blue eyes.

"During the War of 1812, one of your mother's kin was a soldier who fought against the British during their famous attack on the City of Baltimore and Fort McHenry. He and his friends held out inside that old brick fortress despite the terrible bombardment from the Royal Navy that lasted all night long," Daddy said. "A young American named Francis Scott Key was on board one of those British warships to negotiate the release of a prisoner. He witnessed the bombardment and the next morning when he saw the fort's shredded stars and stripes flag still proudly waving in the morning breeze, he wrote a poem called 'The Star Spangled Banner.'"

"Mrs. Powell at school told us that poem became our national anthem," Molly said.

"Then, there was the American Revolution with George Washington," Daddy continued.

"Gosh Daddy, did your family fight in that war too?" Molly asked leaning forward.

"Back then my family were sailors and one of them, Patrick Spence, sailed in a beaten up old ship called the Bonhomme Richard. He was lucky because one of the greatest and bravest sailors who ever lived commanded it... Captain John Paul Jones. In a famous battle, the Bonhomme Richard fought a large English ship named the Serapis for hours. When asked if he wanted to surrender, Captain Jones replied, 'Sir, we have not yet begun to fight.' It turned out that the Americans defeated and captured the British ship, although their beloved Bonhomme Richard sank beneath the waves."

Jimmy asked, "Is all that stuff true, Dad? No fooling?"

"Yes son, it really is."

It seemed then that Molly and Jimmy were beginning to understand why Daddy had to go away for awhile.

"I love you so much Daddy," Molly said while throwing her arms around him. "I guess you really do need to go and help out."

"Our ancestors, those men and women who came before us, made us who we are today. Each generation played their parts and paid their dues, honey. But we're free Americans today because of them and I have been called to do my part. One day it may be yours and Jimmy's turn."

"Don't worry," Molly said while Mom joined the group hug. "We'll make General Washington proud."